THE ART & MAKING OF

SKYDANCE
ANIMATION

SPELLBOUND

THE ART & MAKING OF SPELLBOUND

ISBN: 9781803362434

Published by Titan Books
A division of Titan Publishing Group Ltd.

144 Southwark St.

London

SE1 0UP

FIRST EDITION: NOVEMBER 2024

10 9 8 7 6 5 4 3 2 1

DID YOU ENJOY THIS BOOK?

We love to hear from our readers.
Please e-mail us at: readerfeedback@titanemail.com
or write to Reader Feedback at the above address.

To receive advance information, news, competitions, and exclusive offers online, please sign up for the Titan newsletter on our website: www.titanbooks.com

A CIP catalogue record for this title is available from the British Library.

Printed and bound in China.

THE ART & MAKING OF

SKYDANCE
ANIMATION

SPELLBOUND

RAMIN ZAHED

TITANBOOKS

Fernando López Juárez

Contents

Foreword

Back in January of 2019, when we first embarked on the journey to make *Spellbound*, I felt there was something very noble about the story and the themes that it addressed. We faced the challenging goal of making a fun animated movie that appealed to everyone, but also addressed the emotions that come about when a family is torn apart. As in all good stories, we needed to peel away the many layers to get to the heart of the matter.

I believe that *Spellbound* is a very special movie and it could be one of the best animated films made in a long time, because we approached everything from an honest, emotion-driven point of view. Of course, we also had the gift of Alan Menken and Glenn Slater's wonderful songs, which helped us take the movie to memorable heights.

I feel so fortunate to be working with the incredible team of artists at Skydance Animation, both in the US and in Spain. We all knew that the unique subject of the project had tremendous potential, but it was also going to be one of the most challenging movies of our careers. It was evident that we were working on a movie that would be very meaningful to our audience on many levels. We held the bar quite high in terms of the quality of creativity and imagination. That's why the characters, designs, and environments are a true feast for the eyes. I believe that the world of *Spellbound* is unlike anything we have seen before.

As you thumb through the pages of this book, I hope you'll enjoy this behind-the-scenes look at the movie and appreciate the wonderful art created by the gifted artists who envisioned the characters and magical realm of Lumbria.

BY JOHN LASSETER

Fernando López Juárez

Introduction

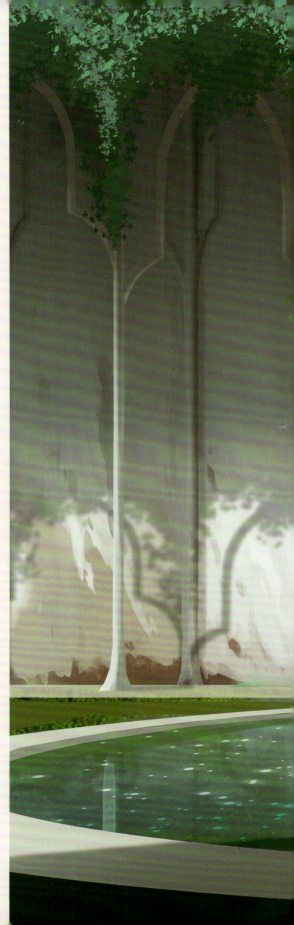

Ever since Walt Disney gifted the world with *Snow White and the Seven Dwarfs* in 1937, spirited young princesses have been familiar figures in animated movies. However, Ellian (voiced by Rachel Zegler), the dynamic new character introduced in *Spellbound*, is definitely not your regular fairy-tale princess. In fact, her enchanting world, unusual dilemma and sweeping adventures truly push the boundaries of what audiences have come to expect in movies set in faraway magical kingdoms.

Ellian faces the seemingly impossible task of reversing a spell that has transformed her parents into giant, destructive monsters. Throughout the movie, she must find out what brought about this change in the beloved king and queen and how she can cure them in order to restore peace in the wonderous kingdom of Lumbria.

One of Skydance Animation's first projects, *Spellbound* is the studio's second animated feature film, following *Luck*, which was directed by Peggy Holmes and released in 2022. The film was produced by the talented teams of artists and technical wizards in Los Angeles and Madrid (at Skydance Animation Madrid, which was formerly known as Ilion Animation Studios).

Like many acclaimed animated films, this colorful fantasy musical went through many evolutions over the past seven years and was originally titled *Split*. *Spellbound* is directed by Vicky Jenson, an animation industry veteran who is best known for directing *Shrek* and *Shark Tale*, as well as production design work on *The Road to El Dorado*. Furthermore, *Spellbound* is produced by John Lasseter, David Ellison, Dana Goldberg, and Bruce Anderson, with a screenplay by Lauren & Elizabeth and Julia Miranda.

In addition to Zegler, *Spellbound*'s stellar voice cast includes Nicole Kidman, Javier Bardem, John Lithgow, Jenifer Lewis, Nathan Lane, and Tituss Burgess. The film's memorable songs are written by eight-time Oscar®-winner Alan Menken (*The Little Mermaid*, *Beauty and the Beast*, *Aladdin*) and Glenn Slater (*Tangled*, *Ralph Breaks the Internet*).

Jenson says she fell in love with the premise of the movie right from the beginning. "As soon as David Ellison and Dana Goldberg pitched me the idea of *Spellbound* back in the fall of 2017, it immediately spoke to me as a story filled with emotion, relevance, and heart. Generally, animated features begin with an idea of the world in which to set the movie. There is this old saying in animation during development: 'The movie will tell you what it wants to be about.' So, it's rare that a story leads with so much meaning and so much to say right from the get-go."

Fernando López Juárez

> Fernando López Juárez

"We were very lucky to have Vicky as director because she started her career as an artist working in production design and art direction," adds executive producer John Lasseter. "She has such a deep passion for the art form, and she was able to lead the Skydance Animation team in such a smart, inventive, and inspired way all throughout the process."

The director says that the unexpected storylines and the unique nature of the characters makes *Spellbound* stand out among other animated fare. "The story doesn't have a traditional fairytale happy ending," Jenson explains. "The princess doesn't quite get what she thought she wanted at the start. But by moving through the question of what makes a family, she grows and discovers a different, but still a true, happiness. It's one based on what 'is' as opposed to some idealized expectation of what 'should be.'"

"One of the first things that we did was to get a deep understanding of the subject matter," says Lasseter. "We had many meetings with Dr. JoAnne Pedro-Carroll, a well-respected psychologist who wrote a book titled *Putting Children First*. She helped us get to a better truth about the experiences of families who go through separation and divorce. As a result, we made this fantasy a deeper journey by using that experience as a metaphor. Ellian's parents are turned into monsters and depicted as gigantic, unruly pets, so she is forced to become the adult of the family, which is what happens to children of divorce. That became our nugget of truth that is buried deep inside the fantasy."

For producer Bruce Anderson, one of the many appealing aspects of the project was that it offers a modern fairy tale set in a very immersive world. "Right from the opening of the movie when you see our main character riding on a gryphon, you realize that you're pulled in this magical world that you would love to escape to right away," he explains. "You know that you have never seen a place or fantastic creatures like these before. As John [Lasseter] put it, this is a place where everyone would love to spend a nice vacation."

Anderson, who joined Skydance Animation after many years at Blue Sky Studios, where he produced hits such as *Ferdinand, Horton Hears a Who!*, and the *Rio* movies, says he is also quite impressed by the way Jenson and her team have been able to balance the fantastic elements of the movie with heartfelt emotions and recognizable real-world conflicts.

"What Vicky has done is quite special because the movie takes us to a very unique place, but it also feels familiar," he says. "We see the world through Ellian's eyes. She has some typical feelings that all teenagers might have about their place in the world. The issues

that the parents are struggling with [are also relatable]. Their challenges are set in a fantasy setting, but [the story] stays contemporary in terms of attitude and the overall fun of it all. Even the general sarcasm that a teenager might have, and has had for several generations in movies, is prevalent in *Spellbound*. Everything is tackled so effectively here that it doesn't feel like it's been seen before."

Jenson describes the film's visual style as "a seamless integration of delicately stylized storybook ideals and aesthetics, as well as fantasy elements, realized in a believable and grounded manner." She says she has always

↘ Julián Romero Muñoz

been inspired by the artists of early Golden Books, especially Mary Blair and Alice and Martin Provensen. "There is a graphic but charming feel to their work, as well as a sophisticated way of handling a lot of rich colors that I love. When I came across two of our main concept artists, the twins Elena and Olivia Ceballos, I recognized kindred spirits and quickly put them to work. They were vital in conceiving our Dark Forest of Eternal Darkness and the ephemeral Lake of Light."

For the film's production designer Brett Nystul, who has worked on projects such as *Minions: The Rise of Gru*, *The Secret Life of Pets*, and *The Croods*, one of the appealing qualities of the production was that it drew inspiration from classic Disney artists like Eyvind Earle and Mary Blair, as well as an eclectic variety of real-world architecture and flora and fauna. "One of the cool things about *Spellbound* is that we had artists from all over the world on our creative team," says Nystul. "Of course, most of them are from Spain, as our studio is in Madrid, but we also have artists from South America, eastern Europe, and Italy. So, the overall look of the movie owes a lot to everybody putting their heads together and evolving in its own special way."

"I think the emotional honesty of the movie really makes it special," says head of story Brian Pimental. "It doesn't shy away from real emotions. I am also proud of the inventiveness of the story and the set pieces and the way it uses a fantasy world in a new way. I hope

the movie will be remembered for the way it shows that life doesn't always follow a straight line: That it's futile to try to hold on to things and the way things were, because everything changes. In the beginning of the movie, Ellian looks at love from a child's point of view, but later, she must accept that love is not always guaranteed. I also love the message that you should always look for the light, even when you are surrounded by darkness."

Jenson echoes this feeling. "There was a concerted effort to not sugarcoat the depth and power of the emotions our characters were feeling. We worked very closely with clinical psychologist Dr. JoAnne Pedro-Carroll who guided us through the issues, stages, and truth of families that go through this difficult time. The last thing we wanted to do was *Parent Trap* the story!"

The director says she's also very grateful for the talented and creative team at the studio for viewing this enterprise as a true labor of love. "Working at Skydance has been an eye-opening and ultimately rewarding experience," she says. "I have been at the start of several new studios, and it is always an incredibly exciting time. But rarely have I experienced a studio who so heartily believed in its future and the value of its artists. I hope audiences will be entertained by our movie and feel this story and recognize the truths at its core—that the love of family can be unbreakable and that the love we share is what keeps us 'spellbound.'"

Fernando López Juárez

Guillermo Ramírez

CHAPTER ONE

Characters

Princess Ellian

It's easy to see that the charming, young princess Ellian is the true emotional heart of the movie. From the very first moment in the film's opening sequence when we meet this energetic 14-year-old princess riding on her gryphon, she makes a big impression as a force to be reckoned with. For the creative team, it was obvious that the heroine of *Spellbound* was going to be likeable, forceful, and quite unlike other feisty princesses of other animated movies.

"Ellian is the character I most relate to," says Jenson. "Not because my parents ever separated, but because I wanted to feel—and have audiences really feel—her emotional growth across the story. There was a real challenge in visualizing and embodying Ellian's inner journey as she moves from being a kid who wants her family back together and the one mature enough to see what really makes a family. The visual of Ellian facing her inner child, a child who just couldn't let go of what used to be, was really important to me. Seeing Ellian comfort and encourage herself was a debated image that ultimately survived the cut!"

As the film's editor, Susan Fitzer, points out, because Ellian's family is going through a transition, this makes Ellian fearful of an uncertain future. "She is very resistant to that transition because of how it might impact her world, and whether she can still be happy and thriving," says Fitzer, who has worked on a wide range of animated movies, including *How to Train Your Dragon* and *Captain Underpants: The First Epic Movie.* "After working on the movie for over five and a half

▸ Final render
◂ Isis Mussenden

Carolina Cuenca García

years, I still get choked up listening to her sing her wonderful song 'What About Me?'. Her situation is relatable not just to a teenager whose family is going through divorce, but to any young person who just wants to be heard, loved, and acknowledged."

Like all interesting movie heroines, Ellian grows and evolves as the result of the events of the movie. "We used to call her a bulldozer with daisies," jokes head of story Brian Pimental. "She's very optimistic, and she's going to make things happen the way she wants to,

and nothing is going to stand in her way. We found a lot of comical ways to play with that. Another interesting thing about her is that her 'I want song' is different from other heroines in the past because she doesn't want to go and explore the world or to have adventures. *The Way It Was Before* expresses that she's simply longing for permanence instead."

Of course, the design team spent a lot of time and effort to make sure the character was uniquely designed and really looked the part. As character designer Guillermo Ramírez

recalls, "She was the first character we designed, and is probably the one that went through the most changes. We wanted to show that she's split between two worlds, so you can see that reflected in her hairstyle—her curly hair is braided on one side and loose on the other. She may still be a girl, but she must grow up fast and act like a queen as well."

Ramírez mentions that the inspiration for the character's look and clothing came from Spain, Morocco, other North African countries, and India. "The movie is inspired by a great

▲ Guillermo Ramírez
◀ Guillermo Ramírez
▸ Adonay Cordero Santana
▾▸▸ Final renders

"She's very optimistic, and she's going to make things happen the way she wants to."

Brian Pimental —
Head of story

blend of cultures and traditions," he says. "There have been so many princesses in animation, so we really wanted a look that was both original and appealing. Her thick eyebrows, curly hair, and skin color are especially common in the region. The proportions evolved, but because she was the first character we designed, it had a big influence on the others as well. The funny thing is that we designed the character before we knew who was going to voice her, and when they told me Rachel Zegler had the part, I was so pleasantly surprised because, just by coincidence, they look a bit similar. They have the same big eyes, black eyebrows, and strawberry-shaped faces!"

Character surfacing supervisor Adina Krause says the most challenging character was Ellian. "Since she was the basis of all the other human characters, we had to figure out how her skin would react to the light, how her eyes should look, and what level of stylization we needed to have," she explains. "Her clothes were also the first ones we worked on, and we really pushed the details of the embroidery on her outfits. We used painting as the base and developed a way to generate the stitching based on painted lines."

➤➤ Carolina Cuenca García
➤ Final render

Flink

Where would an amazing princess be without her funny sidekick? Flink is Ellian's very cute, hamster-like pet, who loves her and truly understands her, and is her stalwart companion. Adorable sidekicks are a familiar staple of animated fairy tales, and it's not surprising that this mysterious, small critter had its own creative evolution to become one of the favorites of the creative team.

The character was originally named Scribbles and its backstory goes back to some drawings by Ellian that had come to life. "He was supposed to be just a bunch of scribbles," says Ramírez. "He went through many changes. At one point, he was the manifestation of Ellian's negative thoughts. His texture was not completely solid—it was all smokey and liquid. But that idea seemed too dark for the movie, so he became more of a rodent-like creature. I had a lot of fun with Flink and ended up

▸ Final render
▾ Guillermo Ramírez

▶ Guillermo Ramírez

putting a lot of my own dog, who was a mix of chihuahua and dachshund, into the design," says Ramírez.

Ramírez says that sometimes, in animated movies, sidekick companions tend to be one-hundred percent cute—but in Flink's case, he wanted to bring some realism into the mix. "That's where using my old dog as reference came in handy. For example, the way Flink leans on one side when he sits, sort of at a weird angle, came from real life. He may be a bit odd and ugly, but still very lovable!"

▸◂ Guillermo Ramírez

◂ Ignacio Pesquera Lopez

Gryphons

The gryphons in *Spellbound* don't quite look like the classic mythological hybrid animals of ancient Greece and Persia, which have the body, tail, and the back legs of a lion, and the head and wings of an eagle. As Ramírez explains, "We wanted to put a new spin on that traditional look," he notes. "Our gryphon has the face of a cheetah with black markings on it and giant owl-like ears. His neck and body are super long, so he kind of looks like a giant ferret with wings. He has a long tail like a fat cat, and the sharp talons of an eagle. We wanted him to look both cute and strong, and we need to believe that he could fly as well. He has a mix of feathers and fur on his chest, which created a complex texture in CG—but the end results are great."

"Who wouldn't want to have one of these as their pet?" adds Lasseter.

◆▶ Final renders

◥ Guillermo Ramírez

Guillermo Ramírez

> "Our gryphon has the face of a cheetah... and giant owl-like ears... he kind of looks like a giant ferret with wings."
>
> *Guillermo Ramírez –*
> *Character designer*

‣ Guillermo Ramírez

‣ Guillermo Ramírez

◂ Adonay Cordero Santana

▲ Guillermo Ramírez   ▲ Carolina Cuenca García   ▲ Guillermo Ramírez

▶ Guillermo Ramírez

▾◥ Guillermo Ramírez

◂ Pablo Alonso Sánchez

Final renders
Guillermo Ramírez

"Who wouldn't want
to have one of these
as their pet?"

John Lasseter —
Executive producer

Carolina Cuenca García

Monster Ellsmere

When Ellian sings "My life's not ideal. There's a few flaws, mainly because my parents are monsters—no, actual monsters, for real!" in the opening song of the movie, we are introduced to the Queen in her transformed state as a pink and green monster. Monster Ellsmere is a tiger-like creature with six legs, two small wings, and a long tail. She has a frog-like tongue with which she can capture prey instantly, and on occasion she is known to use her deadly claws. She is always hungry and loves to devour food, but she absolutely despises water. She loves to stare and appreciate the qualities of the world around her: She might just stare at a rock in front of her for hours. She is described as impatient, aloof, and unforgiving—all the negative qualities of the Queen have become exaggerated and amplified in her monster form.

"I've really come to enjoy all the scenes with the Monster Ellsmere," says Anderson. "I think what our director Vicky Jenson did with her as a character and overall attitude and design is incredible. She can't say much in the first half of the movie, but she does a lot of talking through her actions. She's trying so hard to get back her memories with Ellian, and her emotional journey and physical characteristics are just unique and so much fun to watch on screen. She quickly became my favorite."

As you can imagine, designing a character that was a combination of several animals with two hands and six legs was both a lot of fun and had its share of headaches. As Ramírez recalls, "Because the monsters are imaginary creatures, we could use a wide variety of references in nature, but we always had to make sure they didn't look too aggressive. Vicky did some great sketches as a starting point, and then we experimented with various shapes and animals."

‣ Final render

◆▶ Guillermo Ramírez

One of the key characteristics of the monsters' designs was that although they were clearly otherworldly and somewhat surreal, the audience can clearly recognize the Queen and the King underneath the transformation. "As the director told us, we need to really love these characters because we go on a long journey with them through the movie," says Ramírez. "Even in their altered states, we needed to remember that they are Ellian's parents and they still love and care for her deeply. However, they still need to be menacing enough so that people are afraid of them and the damage that they can do."

Among the many sources of inspiration for Monster Ellsmere was the unusual-looking pink salamander commonly known as the axolotl. "It is simple but also kind of weird. We also needed softness, so we added the feathers and the fur to her body. She also has these goat horns, and a mouth that resembles a bird's beak. Add to that the fact that she has six limbs, and you get a monster that we have never seen before, but when you look at it carefully, it begins to look familiar."

According to Krause, who worked on the surface textures of the monsters, one of the most difficult aspects was their size. "We needed a lot of textures because they are so big, and we had to make sure the resolution and details were correct," she points out. "They also needed to resemble their human counterparts. So, for example, in the Queen's case, she wears a green embroidered outfit that you can see has transformed into the green fur on her monster body.

▴ Carolina Cuenca García
▾ Final render

▴ Carolina Cuenca García

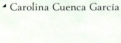

◄▲▼ Carolina Cuenca García

Queen Ellsmere

Ellian's mother, the Queen of Lumbria, was known for being a wise and just ruler before her transformation. Many years ago, her future husband King Solon fell in love with her because of her charming personality, timeless beauty, and contagious appetite for life. While she is also known for her wisdom and balanced approach to life's challenges, she also feels deep emotions and can never forgive the King for his mistakes and for moving on so quickly. Of course, when we first see the Queen in the movie, she has already been transformed into a monster.

To bring this complex and fascinating character to animated life, the creative team continued their quest for bringing dimensionality and interesting physical attributes to the sometimes-predictable role of queens in fairy tales.

In the early days of development, the King and Queen lived in their own separate kingdoms, and this impacted the designs of the characters because each character was shaped to reflect the visual language of their distinct realms. However, as the story evolved, and it was decided that both characters should come from the same territory, the Queen's design also went through a transformation.

‣ Final render
‣ Guillermo Ramírez

▲▼ Adonay Cordero Santana

◥ Guillermo Ramírez

"Originally, she was quite stylized and very thin, but we ended up with a more rounded shape with a beautiful, long nose," says Ramírez. "For inspiration, we looked at a variety of famous Indian actresses. One of our first references was Vidya Balan, and I think you can still see her likeness in the final version of the queen."

Ramírez says that the Queen was one of the most challenging characters to finalize. "This character had a very unique and distinctive face, which was quite appealing as an illustration, but it was not easy to translate into CG animation because, in the end, the design has to work from every angle," he explains. "But all the hard work paid off because I think we ended up creating a very memorable Queen Ellsmere for the movie."

⌃⌃ Guillermo Ramírez

▸ Guillermo Ramírez

▸ Ignacio Pesquera Lopez

▴ Final render
▾ Carolina Cuenca García

Monster Solon

The dark spell that transforms the Queen also turns King Solon into a rambunctious, wild beast. He is described as a cross between a giant gopher, a big bear, and a wild puppy. Oh, and you have to throw in some armadillo in there on account of his scales.

"We wanted him to be able to stand upright like a bear, but we also wanted him to be able to pounce and jump on all fours," says Ramírez. "King Solon wears this embroidered jacket with diamonds on it, so we wanted to replicate that visual on his purple scales as well. There's also some crocodile and dragon reference in the design. If Monster Ellsmere is more like a cat in the way she can swing from a chandelier and

lay down wherever she wants, Monster Solon is like a playful giant dog. So, you can see them as a nice couple together. We made sure that they have that chemistry in monster form as well."

Supervising animator François-Xavier Bologna mentions that the evolution of the Solon and Ellsmere monsters were some of the biggest challenges for him and his team. "These characters have a really big evolutionary arc in the movie," he says. "They are these monsters in the beginning of the movie that are wild animals and

▸ Final render
▴ Guillermo Ramírez

Guillermo Ramírez

need to slowly evolve to regain their humanity. This had to be done in subtle ways because they don't switch suddenly. You can see the transformation in the eyes. When they look at each other or at Ellian more directly, there's perhaps a delicate highlight in their eyes—this was our way of dropping clues so that the audience can see the King and Queen inside those monsters. That was really interesting and important to me as an animator."

❥ Guillermo Ramírez

▲ Adonay Cordero Santana

> "If Monster Ellsmere is more like a cat... Monster Solon is like a playful giant dog."
>
> *Guillermo Ramírez —*
> *Character designer*

King Solon

The ruler of Lumbria, King Solon, has been famous for his good heart and wisdom. He's described as playful, passionate, brave, and spontaneous. He can't stand it when Ellsmere points out his faults or wins an argument, but deep down inside, he still loves her despite their differences. And of course, he always wants to be a good father for Ellian and a just leader for his country.

"For reference, in the beginning, we looked at several Spanish and Moroccan actors. Although we didn't know that Javier Bardem was going to voice the King at first, we used his physical attributes as inspiration," says Ramírez. "We wanted him to be a big and strong character, but not totally athletic and in shape. He needed to look like a dad, with a little bit of a belly. You can imagine that he was a fit soldier when he was a young man, but now he has a comfortable life, so he looks like he is enjoying himself. He needs to be a good authority figure and be respected as a king, but he is also a warm father figure in Ellian's life."

▾ Isis Mussenden   ▸ Final render

▸▸▹ Guillermo
Ramírez

Guillermo Ramírez

Ignacio Pesquera Lopez

◂ Final renders

▴▴ Ignacio
Pesquera Lopez

On Crafting Magical Visuals

For visual effects grooming lead Andres Corón, mixing the feathers and the fur that cover the bodies of Monster Ellsmere and the gryphons, and the dragon-like scales on the Monster Solon offered their share of tricky moments. "Creating these assets was challenging because the feathers and the groom needed to blend together seamlessly, with the exception of the wings, which were only covered with feathers," says Corón. "We had to collaborate closely with the rigging department so that we could apply the right simulations for the feathers. The wings of the gryphons also needed to fold naturally and smoothly. Initially, the gryphons played a smaller role, and they were only used in the background, but as their parts developed and they became more important in the story, we spent more time on them. We had to add wind simulations on their feathers as they fly, so we looked at a lot of footage of eagles in flight as they pan when they're in hunting mode and studied how they fold their giant wings when they landed." Because the film's characters range from tiny (like Ellian's purple pet, Flink) to very large (as in the Monsters and gryphons), the surfacing department had to work carefully to ensure the details matched when they shared the screen together. Krause says, "While the groom department handled the hair on the characters and took care of haircuts and the fur and feather, our task was to give them a base texture with the right colors for the groom."

➤▸ Final renders

Minister Nazara

One of the most powerful people in Lumbria, Minister Nazara is also a caring figure who feels very protective of Ellian. Although at first glance she may seem to be very blunt and all about business and protocol, she will use everything in her power to save the kingdom and keep Ellian out of harm's way. She is different from Minister Bolinar who is sentimental, and that's one of the reasons they often find themselves arguing with each other about the right way to prepare Ellian for the throne since her transformed monster-parents are unable to rule.

According to Jenson, Nazara is one of the characters that went through some of *Spellbound*'s biggest changes. "She used to be the traditional villain of our story," she recalls. "Nazara was originally conceived as Solon's sister, and she was going to be driven by hate against Ellsmere who stole the heart of her brother. There were two kingdoms in the movie, and they had been at war over what was true magic. One was a kingdom of wizards and the other a kingdom of sorcerers."

The look of the character also went through a series of changes. "Nazara is a strong-appearing woman who cares for the princess a lot and wants the best for the kingdom," notes Ramírez. "She started out looking more like an austere Spanish soldier chief. She also looked more like Ellian and Solon, because she was supposed to be King Solon's sister. As the character evolved, it was decided that she didn't have to be related to them anymore, and so we gave her a completely different look. We made her body more slender and her features softer because she wasn't a soldier anymore. We gave her a short, very practical haircut. The point was that she is more concerned about the important details of running the kingdom than her appearance."

▸ Final render

▾ Guillermo Ramírez

Guillermo Ramírez

⬑ Carolina Cuenca García

⬎ Hua Angelica Lin

▸ Carolina Cuenca García
▸ Final render

Minister Bolinar

You can look at Bolinar as the yin to Nazara's yang. They are both ministers in the mythical kingdom of Lumbria, but they are opposites when it comes to the way they approach life. Bolinar is outgoing, larger than life, and expresses his emotions loudly and confidently. He misses life back in the days when things were normal and wishes that he could go back to a time when there weren't so many problems and obstacles in his country. He often clashes with Nazara over how to solve problems and how to run things now that the King and Queen have become uncontrollable monsters.

Ramírez provides his backstory: "He used to be a very serious soldier when he was younger," he says. "The character's designs changed as his personality also shifted in the years that the movie was in development. He was originally supposed to be blind in one eye—at one point, he had a lower eyelid on the left side, possibly as a result of a fight. But we changed his

▸ Carolina Cuenca García
▸ Final render

▸ Carolina Cuenca García
▸▸ Guillermo Ramírez

personality, and he became more jovial and fun. We imagined him to be a very strong, athletic man when he was a young soldier. He's an older man now, but he still has the broad shoulders of his youth, but now he has a big belly. We kept in mind that his design always needed to be in sharp visual contrast with how Minister Nazara might end up looking. He is round and shaped like a liquid droplet, while Nazara is slender and tall."

Bolinar proved to be a challenging character to bring to life for Corón. "He is a big guy who wears this beautifully designed jacket, with long sleeves that need to flow effortlessly," he says. "That took a lot of effort, especially when we see him dancing, because we were working

with three layers of cloth, and there's a big number featuring him. So, we had to develop the rig and push it forward to be able to keep the layers of clothing moving naturally as he dances and turns around. We were quite excited to see the final results."

➤ Carolina Cuenca García
➤ Ignacio Pesquera Lopez

"He is round and shaped like a liquid droplet."

Guillermo Ramírez – Character designer

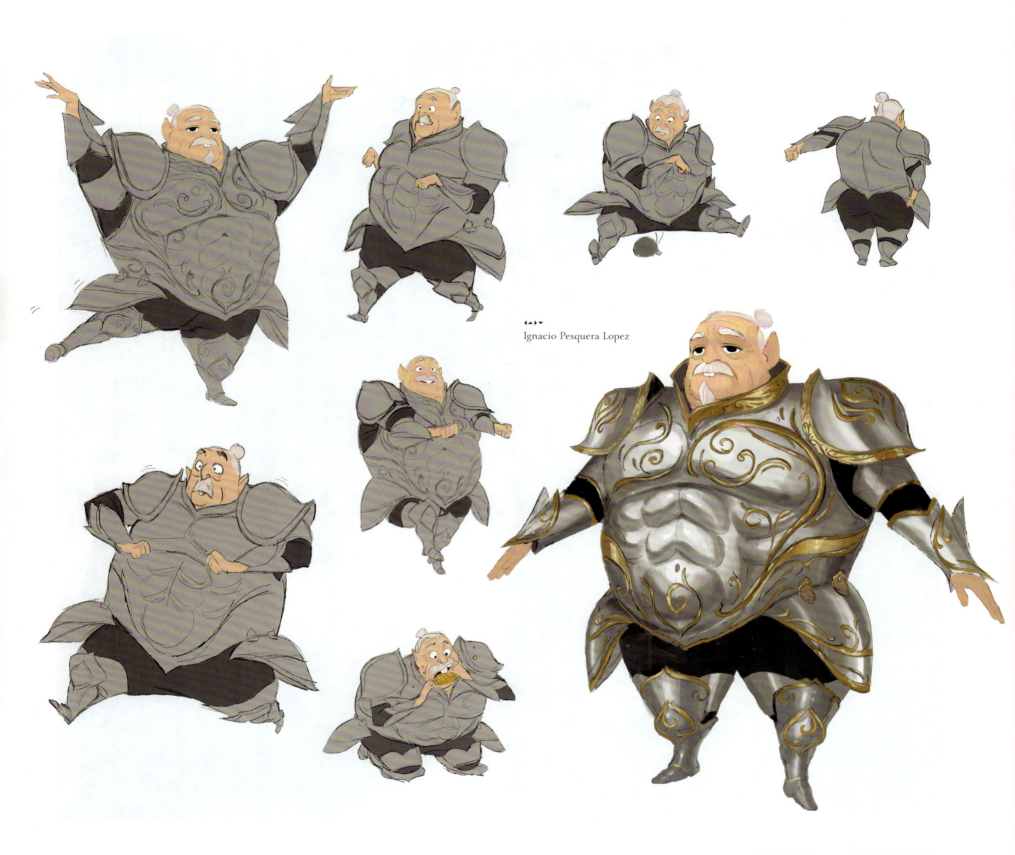

Ignacio Pesquera Lopez

The Old Maid

The Old Maid is one of the few characters in the court who knows the secrets of the King and Queen. As artist Ignacio Pesquera Lopez explains, "Although she is a considerably older and weaker person, the Old Maid is forced to efficiently do a multitude of dangerous and heavy tasks. To underline the irony in the design, it was important that she appeared physically fragile, nervous, and pale. At the same time, she had to have the tenderness of a grandmother somewhere inside her without stepping out of her role at the court or drawing too much attention from her surroundings. The silhouette of the maid is reminiscent of a tassel—this contrasts with the exuberant silhouette of Bolinar, who is someone who seeks pleasure and hedonism."

▸ Final render
▾ Ignacio Pesquera Lopez

▸◂ Ignacio
Pesquera Lopez

▸◥ Final renders

◂ Ignacio Pesquera Lopez

Miscellaneous Characters

According to Ignacio Pesquera Lopez, one of the models for General Cordona was the persistent Samuel Gerard character played by Tommy Lee Jones in the movie *The Fugitive*. "She is always focused and in control of the situation," says the artist. "She takes her work very seriously and almost never strays from the martial spirit that characterizes her."

"The development of this character came at the very final phase of the film," says Lopez. "Therefore, we had many limitations in terms of design. For example, we had to start from a generic character, which limited the originality of her features; she should not have long hair or a ponytail, and her clothes had to resemble the rest of the soldiers as much as possible. We had to find some distinctive elements like the helmet and shield to highlight her rank.

Despite everything, the team did an incredible job and found a very nice balance."

Several guardsmen at the palace were assigned to become "Monster Handlers" after the mysterious transformation of the King and Queen. These brave handlers wear padded outfits and protective garb to allow them to keep Lumbrians from the possible damages that the huge (and often clumsy) monsters might inflict upon them. As artist Carolina Cuenca García explains, "The development of these characters was interesting, from soldiers dressed in whatever they could find to protect themselves from the monster parents' games to versions that have a whole suit of armor especially made for them."

▼ Carolina Cuenca García   ▸ Ignacio Pesquera Lopez

"The development of these characters was interesting, from soldiers dressed in whatever they could find to protect themselves."

Carolina Cuenca García – Artist

▲ Carolina Cuenca García

◄▼ Final renders

The Oracles: Sunny & Luno

Guillermo Ramírez

Sunny and Luno are the tiny, married oracles of the Sun and Moon, respectively, who play a big part in helping Ellian find the solution to returning her parents to their human forms. Voiced by great comedic actors Nathan Lane and Tituss Burgess, they are wonderful comic reliefs that provide a lot of great laughs in the movie. They are the ones who tell Ellian that her parents need to travel through the Dark Forest of Eternal Darkness to break the spell.

Sporting a bushy moustache and rhombus-shaped glasses, Luno is the more pessimistic, "doom-and-gloom-seeing" one. He is a magical

◂ Final render

Guillermo Ramírez

creature who can see into the future. He's also direct, emotionally reserved, and speaks with an Austrian accent. The aptly named Sunny, who wears spectacles, is more happy-go-lucky, wants everyone to follow the light, and feel positive energies. Bald and diminutive, the helpful and funny Oracles are well-meaning characters.

Pimental says he's proud of the fact that he was able to work on bringing wonderful gay characters to animated life for the first time in his career. "The opportunity allowed me to open up a whole different aspect of my personality and to contribute to the creation of these interesting characters," he says. "The idea of having this married gay couple was something that I pushed forward when we started to think that we need a mystical character that could come and help with the parents' situation. At the time, we were also playing with the idea that this magical creature would be a Freud-like therapist. I went to Vicky and told her that it would mean a lot to me if they were a male gay couple because I could contribute in a meaningful way like I had never been able to do in my career."

Pimental says the dynamic between the two Oracles is partially modeled after his own relationship with his partner and those of other long-term married couples on the creative team. "It's all about the loving bickering that goes on between people who have been married for a long time," he notes. "One is optimistic and the other one is grumpier and more negative. Of course, when Nathan Line and Tituss Burgess became the voices for the characters, they really brought them to life with their own special talents and personalities."

Fitzer says some of her favorite scenes in the movie feature the Sun and Moon oracles. "I feel very strongly connected with the evolution of the characters because Brian and I worked together on them very early on. They were thought of as those bickering interlude characters from the movie *When Harry Met Sally*. Then, when we had Brian's drawings, he did the Scratch voice for both characters and really brought them to life. That's when

we realized that they were the key to the fun of the movie. Everything was upped even more when Nathan and Tituss recorded the voices. Nathan Lane did a lot of wonderful improvisation, and I had so many great lines and performances to work with that it was really hard to choose which ones to keep in the final version!"

◢ Guillermo Ramírez

▲ Ignacio Pesquera Lopez

"It's all about the loving bickering that goes on between people who have been married for a long time."

Brian Pimental – Head of story

▲ Ignacio Pesquera Lopez

Ignacio Pesquera Lopez

Ignacio Pesquera Lopez

Lawrence the Frog

The first time we meet the Oracles, they emerge from inside the mouth of a giant frog. Lawrence is another one of the movie's wild and fantastic creatures. He is mainly used to transfer Sunny and Luno to various parts of the Kingdom and to protect them in their home.

The artists had a lot of fun exploring the visual possibilities of this animal character. "At first, the audience might believe that the frog is the true Oracle," says artist Ignacio Pesquera Lopez. "That's why we gave it some subtle magical elements, such as the angler fish antenna which resembles a magician's hat. As for the overall shape, the idea was to make it look like an old vintage yellow taxi. We also had to observe the real world and really figure out what makes a frog look like a frog. For example, learning how frogs insert their eyeballs into their skulls when they blink makes the character funnier and adds credibility at the same time. For the antenna on his head, the idea was to have a bioluminescent light source that changed from green to red—just like a taxi signal.

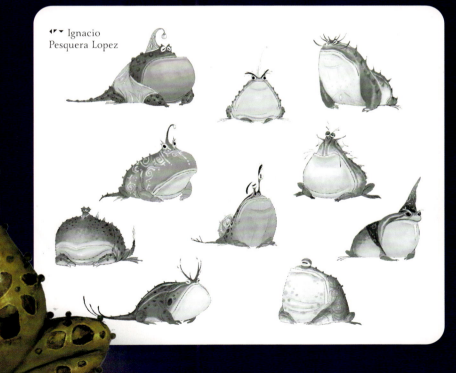

◀▼ Ignacio
Pesquera Lopez

Animals of Lumbria

In addition to the main cast of characters, the magical world of Lumbria is populated by wild creatures that were dreamed up and designed by the artists at Skydance Animation. These fantastic beings were often inspired by real-world animals, which were then transformed as they filtered through the imagination of the project's inventive artists. "The castle, the animals, the Oracles, all the characters might seem familiar on some level, but they are also completely different from things we have seen before," says Lasseter. Magical beasts such as hay dogs, sheep, bush foxes, birds, and rock creatures are sprinkled throughout the land to heighten the mystical wonders of Lumbria.

"We were given the assignment to come up with creatures that could be real," says Ramírez. "This was super fun to do because we could just play around with different shapes. We needed to think of animals that could disguise themselves as plants or rocks or trees. So, you sketch a dog that is made of hay or a desert fox that looks like a bush. These designs went through many iterations and the best ones made the final cut in the movie."

"We also have these beautiful creatures called zellas in the movie, which are sort of like a cross between African antelopes and horses," explains Lasseter. "We wanted these creatures to feel natural in this world, while adding another layer of entertainment to the movie."

◄ Ignacio Pesquera Lopez

◄ Guillermo Ramírez

◄ Michael Sparber

Ignacio Pesquera Lopez

Carolina Cuenca García

Ignacio Pesquera Lopez

Carolina Cuenca García

▾ Ignacio Pesquera Lopez

◢◥ Carolina Cuenca García

Ignacio Pesquera Lopez

Pablo Alonso Sánchez

CHAPTER TWO

Locations

Lumbria

▸ Fernando López Juárez

Welcome to Lumbria, the dazzling, bucolic realm of King Solon and Queen Ellsmere. The magnificent backdrop for the events of the movie is described as the kind of destination at which you'd love to spend a rejuvenating holiday, early retirement, or even a lifetime. While the overall visuals of this realm were inspired by the geography and architectures of countries such as Spain, Greece, and Morocco, animation fans will also notice the strong influence of iconic Disney artists Mary Blair (*Alice in Wonderland, Peter Pan*) and Eyvind Earle (*Sleeping Beauty, Lady and the Tramp*).

As Nystul recalls, early in the development stages the King and the Queen each had their own separate castles and realms, and each realm had its own unique style. "[In the end], we took elements of each of those and combined it to one single architectural style," he says. "Our director, Vicky Jenson, is a huge fan of some of the old Disney artists, and that was a huge draw for me. But it wasn't just doing this for the nostalgic aspect of it: We were also bringing it to the modern age."

Jenson also mentions that fascinating evolution of Lumbria. "The first script I read was certainly epic," she notes. "For instance,

▸ Fernando López Juárez

Santiago Fuentes &
Pablo Alonso Sánchez

there were *three* kingdoms! Ellian's mother, Queen Ellsmere's kingdom, her father, King Solon's kingdom, and the one they had built together while they were happily married. While this was an attempt to recreate, in a fantasy world, the idea of a kid going back and forth between [the homes of] her separated parents and missing her childhood home, it quickly became unwieldy. We finally settled on one kingdom—Lumbria—which was originally Ellsmere's home kingdom."

Once the kingdoms had merged, then came the job of homogenizing its look and feel. "We placed a lot of importance on the details of this kingdom," says John Lasseter. "I knew that we wanted this world to be quite beautiful and unlike any place we had seen in other movies. There have been a lot of fantasies and adaptations of fairy tales and folk tales with princesses and castles, but we wanted this world to be different from anything we had seen before. We have this castle that is incorporated

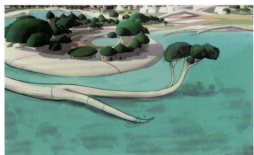

into the barks of the tree, and then you have a giant waterfall around it as a moat."

"In the case of Lumbria, the most important thing was to convey the feeling that vegetation was not simply decorative: vegetation is the very structure of the city, it organizes spaces and influences the way of life of its inhabitants," adds head of final layout Dalia Gutiérrez Aranda. "Lumbria's shape language is made of soft lines that contrast with more graphic rounded masses within which the vegetation is integrated. The challenge was to achieve

▲ Santiago Fuentes & Pablo Alonso Sánchez

Santiago Fuentes &
Pablo Alonso Sánchez

expressive silhouettes without sacrificing naturalness and organic shapes."

"We were inspired by the Moorish architecture of southern Spain and the Arabic influence of Morocco," says Lasseter. "The combination of the historic material with the organic shape of the trees and the roots is quite striking and unusual."

Nystul adds, "One of the best parts of creating Lumbria was how the village grew and evolved as we brought in various Spanish and Moroccan elements. It's a nice white village reminiscent of what you would see in Andalusia in southern Spain or the Greek islands—especially with the crystal-clear, green-blue water in its proximity. We had artists from all over the world working on the movie, and of course most of them are from Spain, and we drew heavily from that region, but we also had artists from South America and all over Europe. So, as everyone put their heads and talents together, it created its own style and artistic flavor."

◄◄ Michael Sparber

Santiago Fuentes & Pablo Alonso Sánchez

Castle

The home of the royal family, we first get our glimpses into the castle during Ellian's opening song. Obviously, the home of Ellsmere and Solon has gone through a drastic transformation after the King and Queen turned into monsters. As Nazara and Bolinar point out in song, "Half the castle's unrepairable, we're in total disarray. Where we once had charm and style and grace and elegance, now we're babysitting elephants!"

One of the most unusual aspects of this Lumbrian castle is its organic architecture and the fact that it is built on the roots of a tree, just like the rest of the houses in the village.

As Nystul points out, "As it goes from the ground level upward, it becomes more architectural, and we get more details and designs. The roofs are actual tree canopies that cover the village homes as well."

▲ Julián Romero Muñoz

◢◥ Iuri Lioi   ◣ Iuri Lioi   ◂ Julián Romero Muñoz

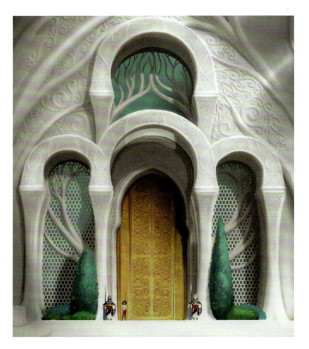

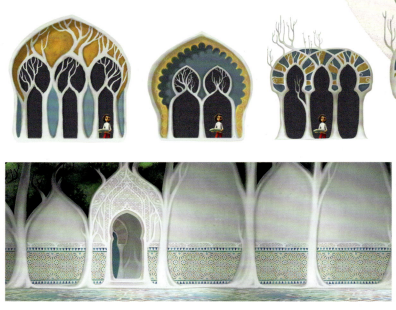

▼ Color key

Fernando López Juárez

Ellian's Bedroom

▶ Fernando López Juárez

Although Ellian is a sensitive young girl who is not materialistic and pretentious, the creative team felt that, because she lives in a huge castle, it would be strange if her room was tiny. "Her mom and dad are the King and Queen of the country, and it just felt weird to give her a tiny room," says Nystul. "It's a good-sized bedroom for a teenager. I remember spending weeks on that and considering things like 'Does the bed grow out of the wall, from the roots?' and 'What kind of furniture does she have in her room?'

But we leaned towards simplicity. She loves riding her gryphon, so there are trophies from races that she might have been in. Obviously, there's no TV or electronics, but she has books and drawings. We created this nice reading nook by the window for her. So, the idea was to create a space for her that was a lot of fun for a teenager, but not overwhelming."

▲◀▶▼ Pablo Alonso Sánchez

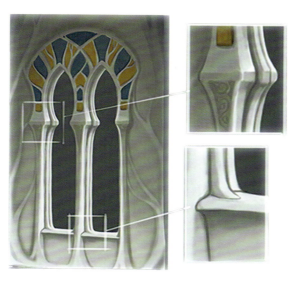

Pablo Alonso Sánchez

"We created this nice reading nook by the window for her. So, the idea was to create a space for her that was a lot of fun for a teenager, but not overwhelming."

Brett Nystul – Production designer

Fernando López Juárez

Family Room

The castle's family room is the place where the young princess and her parents shared many happy moments together before the darkness shattered their world. "This is where the three of them gathered and read books," says Nystul. "There's a huge globe where they used to point to and recall their travels together. Ellian learned how to play the piano in this room. Just walking into this room brings back a warm flood of happy memories of her time with her mom and dad before they became monsters."

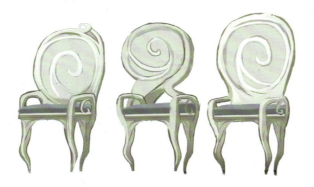

◥ Pablo Alonso Sánchez

The Family Quarters

Once you leave that hall area, even farther up the tree, you come to the family quarters. This is where the family room is. There's a big courtyard between the family room and the parents' quarter. It's thousands of feet up in the sky and there is an amazing view of the village and the mountains. In a lot of ways, it was designed to meet the story needs, but it also just made practical sense. The Great Hall is a bit lower, while the family quarters are quite high so most people won't be able to get to this level.

▾⏴ Fernando López Juárez

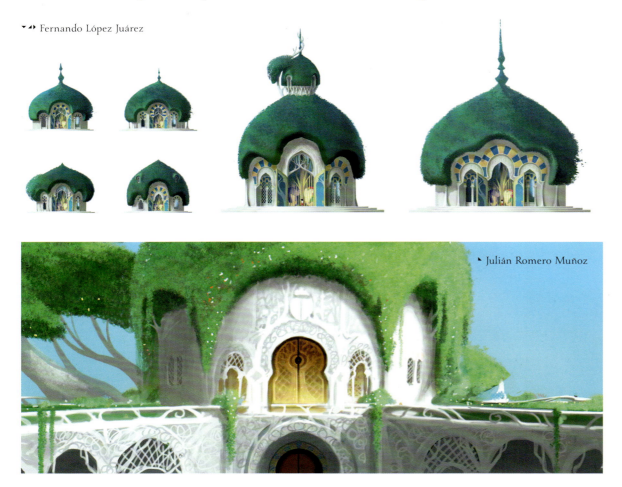

▸ Julián Romero Muñoz

Fernando López Juárez

The Great Hall

You enter the castle through these giant doors, and you go up these long stairs to a green waiting area and you enter the Great Hall, and this is open to everyone in the village. They are allowed to visit and it's a great community center. There's no ceiling and you can see the sky overhead. It's all fed by the sunlight. This is also the site of all the royal parties, including Ellian's birthday. But now that the parents are monsters, they must close those doors and keep the villagers away from the hall.

"The Great Hall was a challenge for all of us, as we had to fill the entire space with vegetation in a subtle and elegant way," says Aranda. "Whilst making the green areas enhance the composition of the shots by contrasting them with the light bark surfaces."

➤ Julián Romero Muñoz
➤ Fernando López Juárez
↩ Santiago Fuentes

Fernando López Juárez

The Castle's Garden

Like many of the other locations in the movie, the garden (and the plants in it) follows a spiral pattern. Nystul explains, "We see this motif as the tree grows in a spiral, and the roads leading up to the castle also have this shape. Once you begin to get to the top level of the village, you are led to this big ramp up to the front of the castle. Just before the ramp, we see the huge family gardens, which has its own pond. This is where Ellian learned how to ride her gryphon as well. Beyond it, it's a typical castle garden!"

"The Lake of Light Mountain also spirals itself to its peak, and you can see this on the flower fields, which are not laid in linear rows—they're also spiral-shaped. Everything has a little bit of curve, and even the trees on the hills have these very sensual patterns to them. We simply followed the Golden Ratio." The Golden Ratio refers to naturally repeating patterns that can be seen throughout nature, from snowflakes to animal shells. "The [resulting] spiral pattern is pleasing to the eye. It just made sense that if we have a castle growing from nature, everything around it would follow this spiral shape as well."

➤ Francis Boncales

The Houses of Lumbria

Houses in Lumbria blend in smoothly with the natural world around them. The white walls and golden doors of the houses in Lumbria are reminiscent of similar villages in Greek islands like Santorini, the Andalusia region in Spain, or small towns in southern France.

When surfacing supervisor David Domingo Jiménez looks back at the many tasks he had to accomplish for the movie, the one that stands out in his mind is working with the white bark that is used in most of the buildings and the castle in Lumbria. "That was a challenge because we had to create it procedurally, and it was very complicated to do, and it's used everywhere in the city," he notes. "Another aspect of the movie that was quite special is that we wanted the look to be reminiscent of Disney's *Bambi*. We were going for this technique in art that is called *sfumato*, which softens the transition between colors. We played with the shadows and the normal versions of the assets to achieve a watercolor feeling. So, for example, in a scene where you have lots of trees, you don't see every single leaf. You only see a patch of blurry green. That was very special for me because it was the first time in my career that I was able to do something like this."

▸ Fernando López Juárez

▸ Santiago Fuentes
▸ Fernando López Juárez

"We played with the shadows and the normal versions of the assets to achieve a watercolor feeling."

David Domingo Jiménez —
Surfacing supervisor

Santiago Fuentes

The Open-Air Market and its Spice Carts

The real-world model for the open-air market in Lumbria are the markets and souks in Marrakesh. Packed with exotic spices and goods and people, the atmosphere, sights, smells, and sounds can transport you to another world. "You can find fresh fish, vegetables, plates, baskets, souvenirs, and clothes in these open-air markets," says Nystul. "It's quite reminiscent of a Moroccan mountain marketplace, where you have these colorful canopies selling all kinds of hand-crafted baskets and food."

Lumbria's economy revolves around trade, and many of the village residents make their living by growing and selling goods at the market. They grow flowers and make baskets. The spice carts also helped the artists balance the white walls with sparks of color and a touch of Lumbrian homegrown flavors.

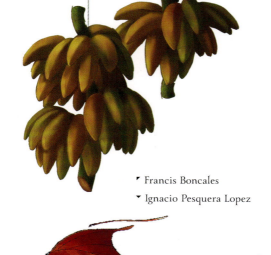

▸ Francis Boncales
▾ Ignacio Pesquera Lopez

▸ Ignacio Pesquera Lopez

▴ Francis Boncales

▴▾▾ Francis Boncales

"It's quite reminiscent of a Moroccan mountain marketplace, where you have colorful canopies."

Brett Nystul —
Production designer

Francis Boncales

The Dock and the Boats

Because Lumbria is surrounded by water, it makes sense that its residents use their boats to enter and exit. Nystul says working on the designs of the wharf and the boats was a wonderfully rewarding and enjoyable assignment.

"Water plays a huge role in the lives of the Lumbrians," he notes. "One of the ways to transport their goods in and out of this world is by boat. There's a huge river that leads up to the castle. They don't need huge ships for their day-to-day needs. These are just regular boats. They bring to mind the scenic waters of Venice, Italy."

→ Fernando López Juárez

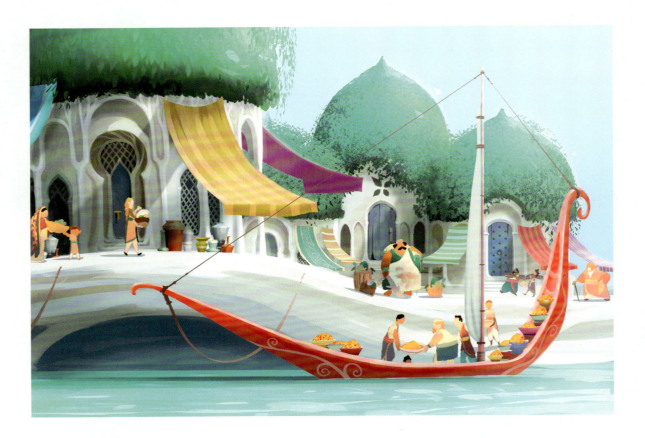

The Great Escape

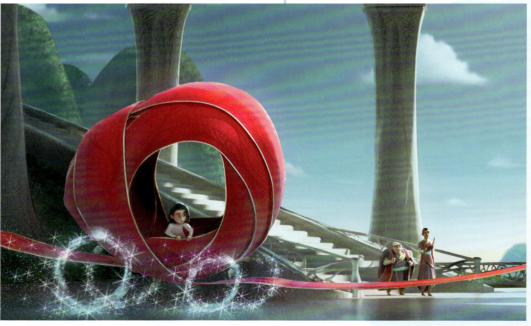

Michael Sparber

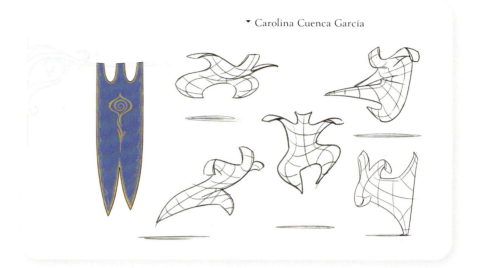

Carolina Cuenca García

Michael Sparber

Michael Sparber

Michael Sparber

The Farmlands

One of the attractive aspects of life in Lumbria is that it has a warm climate. In fact, the weather is so idyllic that the buildings don't even have windows. As Ellian and the other characters begin their trek across the countryside, one of the first things they encounter is the farmland region. "We have these farmhouses that are next to the rice paddy fields, which are filled with water," says Nystul. "There are these big splashes of green and white, and we added more color with the flower fields. The poppy fields are very similar to the ones you may find in the Netherlands. You can also spot some windmill houses. Some of them are standing on stilts, even though they are also grown out of roots and trees. They still have some architectural details on them."

→ Fernando López Juárez

The Dark Forest of Eternal Darkness

Ellian learns from the Oracles that the Dark Forest played a key role in her parents' transformation. This destination is described as "the most treacherous place," and as Luno the Oracle tells her, "It's so dark they named it twice!"

"The forest feels like a cavern of 300-feet-tall sequoia trees with huge trunks," says Nystul. "The darkness is quite overpowering and, at times, we get little glimmers of light coming through the holes in the canopy. The ground is completely covered in a thick layer of moss, which is quite a contrast with the flower fields. You could say it's quite spooky. You can see the Mary Blair influence once again as she was an expert at layering pieces to help create depth. We have layers of black appearing behind the trees, and then you have the vegetation in front of the trees."

As the parents begin to change and they start to communicate better with each other and with Ellian, the total darkness of the forest

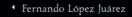

‹ Fernando López Juárez
› Iuri Lioi
▾ Final render

Elena & Olivia Ceballos

Jean-Brice Dugait

Fernando López Juárez

Fernando López Juárez

also begins to give way to more light. We see more light shining through the canopy and there are more colorful flowers and vegetation along the way. In fact, there's a dead tree that separates the darker part of the forest from the brighter and more colorful section, which reflects the shift in the parents' state.

The forest presented its own share of design challenges for the team. "The problem is that you have these giant sequoias in this forest, and imagine putting ten of them across the screen," explains the production designer. "All you would see are the trunks, because the treetops are super high, and we need to focus on the characters on the ground. However, we were able to figure out how to visualize it by adding some new growth and elements to help with the scale."

"In the Dark Forest, the biggest challenge for the team was to create vegetation that was both graphically appealing, natural, and technically efficient for all possible scales," concurs Aranda. "From general shots to those where someone as small as Bolinar (in Flink's body) interacts with nature. Flink's close-ups were enriched with the finest level of detail."

▲▲ Fernando López Juárez

> "The forest feels like a cavern of 300-foot-tall sequoia trees with huge trunks. The darkness is quite overpowering and, at times, we get little glimmers of light coming through holes in the canopy."
>
> *Brett Nystul – Production designer*

◤ Michael Sparber

◤ Julián Romero Muñoz, Michael Sparber, Fernando López Juárez & Raul Morales

Fernando López Juárez

Fernando López Juárez & Michael Sparber

The Oracles' Home

The Oracles' home is in the center of the forest. According to Nystul, their home is cleverly built inside an owl's nest. "They live in a nest, and their home has a Shire-like vibe to it," Nystul says. "The door is almost round. The house lights up like a little jewel in the middle of the darkness that surrounds it. It also signals the beginning of Ellian's journey to follow the light."

↘ Raul Morales
↙ Jean-Brice Dugait

Jean-Brice Dugait

Sea of Sand

Visual effects supervisor Vanitha Rangaraju-Ramanan says one of the most challenging scenes in the movie involved Ellian's journey across a sea of sand. "In this memorable scene, we see her facing a sea of sand as she looks at a beacon very far away," she notes. "Ellian needs to cross this large desert-like land, which changes form and turns into an ocean when there's shadow over it. So, we were tasked with creating this watery-sandy landscape, which becomes extremely turbulent when clouds of darkness swirl over it. This was super difficult to achieve because we had to combine multiple elements so that they behaved in a completely different way, while creating something that didn't feel like anything we've seen before."

Another big task for the effects team was the sequence in which sounds take self-perpetuating physical shapes and turn into either calming, blue-wavey manifestations or angry, jagged red patterns. "Initially, the happy thoughts were going to turn into a bubble-like shape, but eventually they became more of a soothing ripple that kind of resembled a jellyfish," says Jones. "This was one of those instances that the more we played with the idea, the more spectacular it became. We could have taken many different approaches. Just like the rest of the movie, we were trying to avoid hyper-real visuals. Overall, we liked to add our own *Spellbound* style to everything, whether it was taking some octaves off the noise or adding a little extra swirl here and there. Everything had to be consistent with the overall Lumbria vibe."

"The sea of sand was an artistic and technical challenge as the stones were an active part of the sequences," says Aranda. "The interdepartmental synergy with Effects, Animation, and Lighting made the final result possible."

‣ Michael Sparber

Raul Morales

Canyon

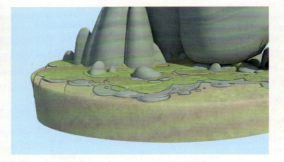

◤◤▶ Fernando López Juárez

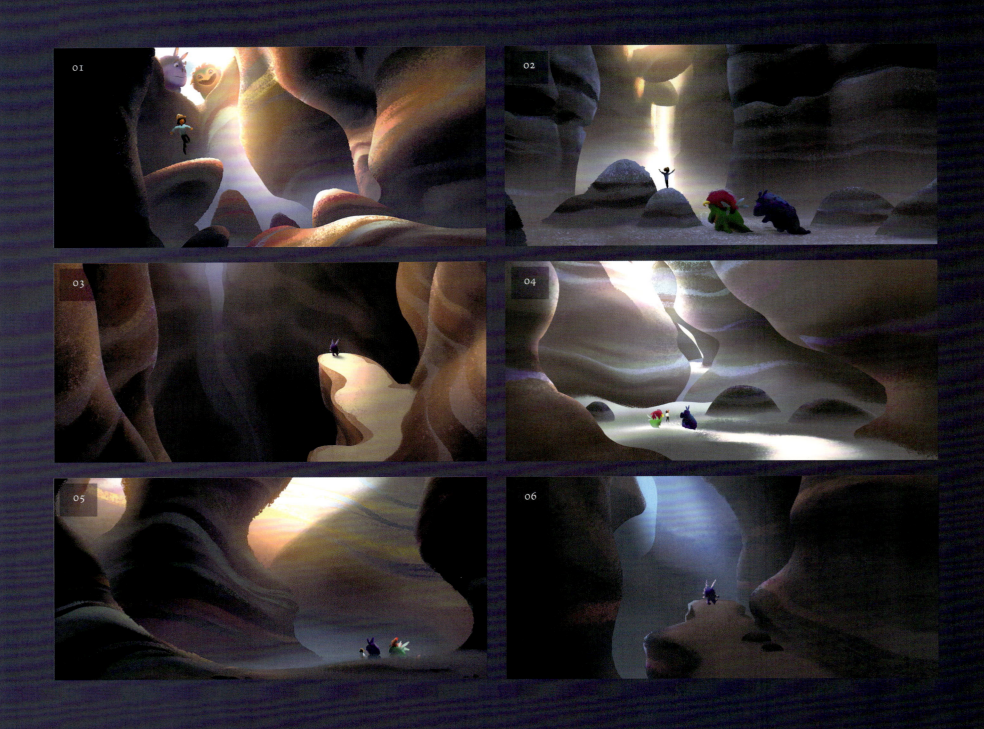

07

Jean-Brice Dugait

Land of the Flinks

◥ Jean-Brice Dugait

▲ Michael Sparber
▼ Santiago Fuentes

Ignacio Pesquera Lopez
Azul Eberhard Carvajal
Carolina Cuenca García

Gryphons' Rookery

As you would expect, the gryphons' rookery must be located at the highest point of Lumbria's tallest mountain. "It's way up in the clouds and touching the sky," says Nystul. "There's a green field covered in tall grass that blows in the wind. Because gryphons fly, and they are huge animals, we knew that they needed a peaceful, idyllic place to rest. Another key point was that Ellian and her mom and dad get a glimpse and understanding of what a family is by observing how the parents take care of their cubs."

Nystul says the objective was to create a warm and inviting air, like a nice grassy meadow on top of the mountain. "Imagine the high cliffs in Ireland, where you have green fields and beautiful wildflowers growing. You can definitely feel the Miyazaki influence here, with the greens and the blues."

For the gryphons' rookery, the importance was the emotional weight of the moment," adds Aranda. "The tall grass made the characters feel embraced and, for a moment, they were a family again. The grass is combed in every shot to help the composition of the characters."

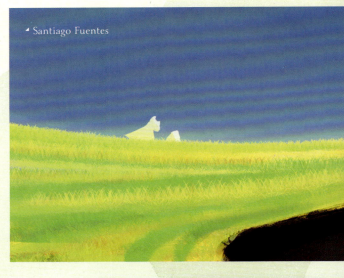
▸ Santiago Fuentes

▾ Elena & Olivia Ceballos

Betty Sourigues

Santiago Fuentes

The Last Mountain

"How do we make it truly breathtaking and iconic?" That was the question on the artistic team's minds as they set out to design and create the Last Mountain. Nystul and his team looked at seven or eight of the most famous mountains in the world, including the Matterhorn and Everest. The design went through a few iterations until the team felt like they had nailed it. If the viewer looks carefully at the peak of the mountain, you will recognize three giant rock formations. "They actually look like three hands," says Nystul. "You may not notice them at first, but at second glance, you will see that there's a spiral shape that leads up to three giant stones that look like hands. They represent the King, the Queen, and Ellian."

➤ Julián Romero Muñoz
➤ Elena & Olivia Ceballos

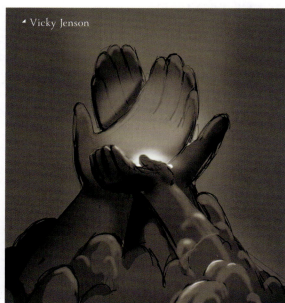

▲ Vicky Jenson

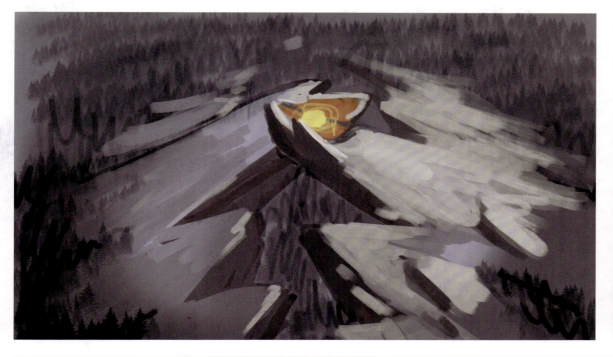

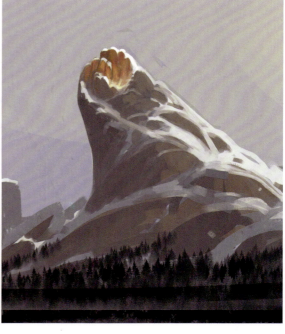

Julián Romero Muñoz

Fernando López Juárez

The Lake of Light

Ellian and her parents are told that the Lake of Light has magical powers to fight the darkness and reverse the spell that made monsters out of the king and queen. This isn't really so much a lake as it is a shimmering, paper-thin layer of light creating what *feels* like the surface of a lake, floating above the ground. "The lake has a certain magical energy to it," says Nystul. "It's not quite liquid, and when Ellian walks through it, it feels like she's walking through oil because she can push it out of the way. She can also pick up these little strands of iridescence. The inspiration came from glowing algae on the ocean surface, like the water in Hawaii or the tropics. When Ellian touches the water, it sparkles and creates these magical particles. This is where truths are told. It's not electrical or forbidding. In fact, it's quite inviting and draws you in with a welcoming force."

"The challenge with the lake's surface was that it needs to feel like both liquid and a thin sheet of light," says effects supervisor Ben Jones. "We wanted it to feel like a nice, calming, and almost gas-like element that has very fluid motions. It also needed to interact correctly with the characters. We looked at some caustic effects, like when sunlight is refracted through the bottom of a sphere. Using that patterning, we broke apart different color channels so the viewer could see some spectrum of lights in different areas, and it was quite beautiful."

Elena & Olivia Ceballos

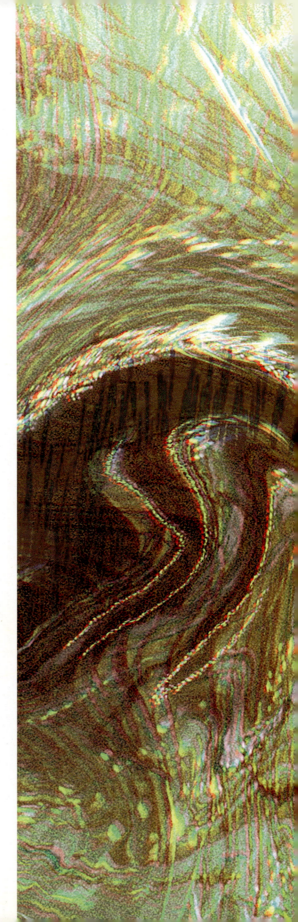

> "The challenge with the lake's surface was that it needs to feel like both liquid and a thin sheet of light."
>
> *Ben Jones — Effects supervisor*

Julián Romero Muñoz

Anatomy of a Scene:
The Way It Was Before

One of *Spellbound*'s pivotal scenes, which really sets the tone for the movie, takes place during the first act, in which Ellian runs through the castle remembering her life before her parents' transformation.

"What's great about this sequence is that everyone can relate to Ellian in a different way because it's so multi-layered and emotional," says John Lasseter. "We all have longed for things and moments in our lives that are gone

forever. As the song is performed visually, it becomes all about her longing for her parents to come back. We decided to use the concept of flashbacks as the memories manifest themselves to her. Brian [Pimental] came up with a lot of the concepts and storyboarded this sequence himself and worked very closely with our director, Vicky [Jenson]. Those two really conceived it together."

"I think what makes the sequence stand out is its sincerity and heart," explains Brian

‣ Michael Sparber
‣ Brian Pimental

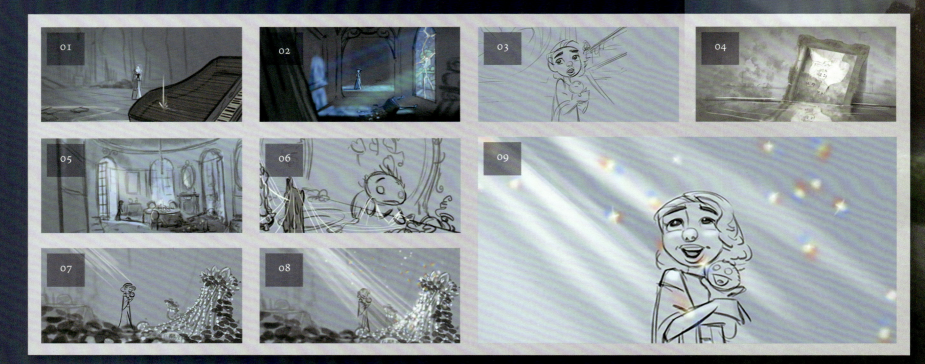

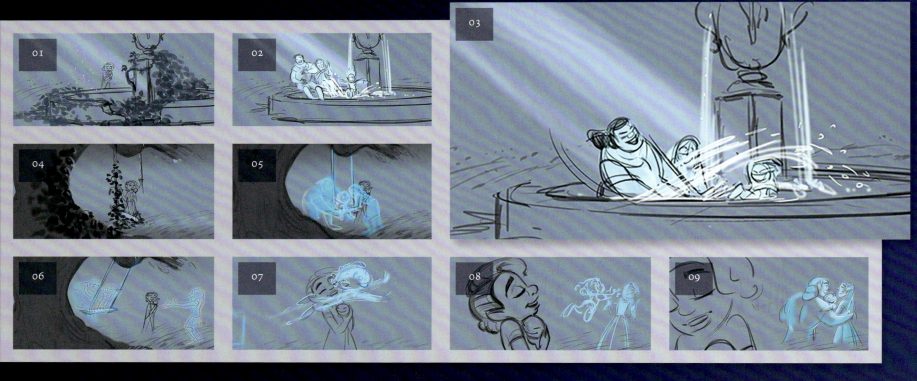

Pimental. "At this point in the story, Ellian is faced with the possibility that her parents might never change back to their human selves. She fears she will be alone for the rest of her life. She longs for the days when her world was simpler, when she was cared for and supported."

He adds, "I love that it is not a typical 'I want' song. Most of the time, a main character will sing about something they long for in the future. Ellian is longing for something she lost and desperately wants to get it back."

"Brian captured brilliantly the intricate essence of this song in his original storyboards," says Vicky Jenson. "We never strayed far from his first drawings! He asked all of us (writers Elizabeth Martin and Lauren Hynek and our amazing editor Susan Fitzer and myself) to share some of our sweetest memories of childhood so that he might find the resonant images that he ultimately created for this sequence. What I love is how Brian managed to make these images meld with the song so seamlessly and effortlessly."

Jenson points out that Ellian comes into the song hurt as she walks through the ruins of her home and feeling the weight of the future without family. "As she remembers the simple moments spent with her parents, she is able to come through strengthened by the memory of

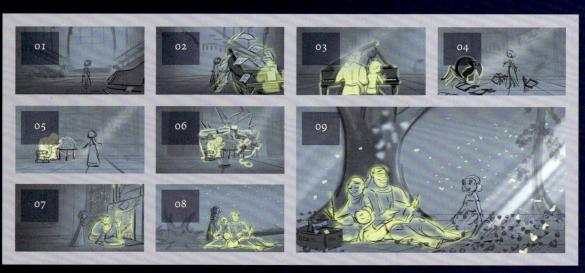

Brian Pimental

that shared love," she notes. "So even as the song seems bittersweet, it is ultimately uplifting."

As Brett Nystul points out, the sequence helps establish the general family dynamics between Ellian and her parents before they became monsters. "It shows Ellian's memories of her growing up with lots of laughter and love between her and her parents," he says. "It's also the first time we get to understand her life before they became monsters. We empathize with her plight now and understand her ache for the old days. The scene is kind of like walking into your childhood family home that is now empty of furniture and pictures,

because the house just sold. The house and walls are the same, but there are no voices and laughter. There is only a cold echo from the empty walls creating a sadness."

Because this important sequence is told through a song, one of the big challenges was to get the correct visual beats to match and sync with the verses in a timeline that clearly shared what was needed visually. "We also wanted to clearly define memories with warmth while keeping the cold austere lonely feel as she travels through the castle rooms and garden," recalls Nystul. "At first, the memories are fleeting in a blueish glow, but as Ellian starts to grasp more

of them, they become more a golden glow of warmth and saturation. We see her loneliness caused by this major disruption and feel her ache for the days before. I think many of us, when times are tough, sometimes remember warm memories with a desire or wish to have that same kind of experience today."

Jenson adds, "There were many technical challenges in realizing this sequence, like the sweeping shot that combines present-day Ellian in her destroyed home while simultaneously showing memories of happier times in that same room. This was one shot that probably took the longest to accomplish.

But honestly the biggest challenge was finding the right balance between nostalgia and celebration. The song and imagery could have easily slipped into melancholy and regret. It's a credit to all the artists involved to find the joy in this yearning, the celebration in remembering, allowing us to cheer for Ellian as she regathers strength, buoyed by the love she feels in these seemingly lost moments." Art director Michael Sparber also points out that Ellian has different types of emotional lows at different parts of the movie. "At her big emotional low in the third act she's mostly angry. In 'The Way It Was Before' sequence, she's obviously sad. Her anger hasn't surfaced yet, but she's holding it in, and that's important to show."

Sparber says it was a fun challenge to think about how to define the color and light differences between those two emotional states. "We played this sequence as dark, moody, soft and cool," he says. "We looked for opportunities to have single light sources that only illuminate the area around her, making Ellian feel alone. For interior shots, she's holding a lantern. Whereas for exterior shots, she's lit under a theatrical spotlight while the rest of the world falls away into darkness. All this sets up the emotional peak in the third act of the film to feel very different with its angry red and contrasted lighting."

Creating a clear past for Ellian was also one of the key challenges of this number. "I had to invent a life for her," says Pimental. "I tried to

set up things we could see again later in the movie, like looking at the stars, or swinging on the swing. My favorite moment was where she was swinging on the gate with her younger self. For me that said it all! She just wants to be carefree like she once was. I had another similar moment where she sang face to face with her younger self. It got cut, but it became the basis for the end of 'What About Me?' when she sang to her younger self there. I was very proud of that moment and glad we brought it back."

Editor Susan Fitzer says the scene allows the audience to really identify with Ellian as it shows viewers the tender moments that have been stolen from her life. "We see her heartbreaking sense of longing and desperate hope that her family might one day be restored," she says. "It is during this song that we truly feel what Ellian has lost. We, the audience, fall in love with Ellian during this sequence and are ready to follow her on any journey that will get her parents back."

Fitzer says she loves the way the sequence illustrates the heroine's memories. "At first these memories of young Ellian and her parents are represented in cool tones that only the viewer sees," she explains. "But after the pivotal lyric 'and we could be together there right now,' the shadow of young Ellian runs right through her older self, and as she does, her image turns from blue to gold. It so effectively conveys the emotion of the entire sequence—a young lady saddened by the distance of her happy childhood but momentarily heartened by the thought that it could return. I'm sure I've watched this moment a hundred times over the past four years, but it still always makes me tear up."

↖ Elena & Olivia Ceballos

Acknowledgments

I am so grateful to the brilliant artists and creative team at Skydance Animation for giving me such a first-class behind-the-scenes tour of *Spellbound*. A huge thank you to Bruce Anderson, Dalia Gutiérrez Aranda, François-Xavier Bologna, Andres Corón, David Domingo Jiménez, Carolina Cuenca García, Susan Fitzer, Vicky Jenson, Ben Jones, Adina Krause, John Lasseter, Ignacio Pesquera Lopez, Brett Nystul, Brian Pimental, Guillermo Ramírez, Vanitha Rangaraju-Ramanan and Michael Sparber. A special thanks to the amazing Helen Rodas Escobar for using her magical powers to make everything run smoothly and on schedule, Titan Books' talented designer Kerry Lewis and to editor extraordinaire/wizard of words, Frankie Piscitelli. The book is dedicated to my terrier sidekick, Gizmo the wonder dog.

- Fernando López Juárez